Published in 2013 by The Rosen Publishing Group, Inc.
29 East 21st Street, New York, NY 10010

Photo Credits: **KEY** tl=top left; tc=top center; tr=top right; cl=center left; c=center; cr=center right; bl=bottom left; bc=bottom center; br=bottom right; bg=background

CBCD = Corbis PhotoDisc; CBT = Corbis; DT = Dreamstime; iS = istockphoto.com; SH = Shutterstock; TF = Topfoto; TPL = photolibrary.com

front cover bg iS; bl TPL; **back cover** cl iS; bl SH; **1**c, cl, cr SH; **2–3**bg TPL; **4–5**bg TPL; **6**bc SH; **7**bc iS; tc SH; **8**bl, br, c, cl iS; **9**tl Gl; bc, bl, cr iS; **10**bl SH; **10–11**bg iS; **11**cr DT; **14**bl, cl SH; **14–15**tc, c SH; **15**cr, tr CBT; bl, cl, tl SH; **16**tl CBT; tr SH; **17**cr CBT; bl DT; br, tl TPL; **18**b SH; **19**c TPL; **20**bl, c; iS; cl SH; **20–21**bc iS; **21**tr iS; cr SH; **22**cl TPL; **24**cl iS; bc TF; **25**c SH; **26**c TPL; **27**bl, cr TPL; **28**bl iS; **28–29**c CBT; tl, bl TPL; **30**bg CBCD; br, tr iS; **32**bg SH

All illustrations copyright Weldon Owen Pty Ltd. **12–13**, **22**tr, br, **23**tl, tr, cl, cr Lionel Portier

Weldon Owen Pty Ltd
Managing Director: Kay Scarlett
Creative Director: Sue Burk
Publisher: Helen Bateman
Senior Vice President, International Sales: Stuart Laurence
Vice President Sales North America: Ellen Towell
Administration Manager, International Sales: Kristine Ravn

Library of Congress Cataloging-in-Publication Data

Close, Edward.
  What do we do with trash? / by Edward Close. — 1st ed.
     p. cm. — (Discovery Education: the environment)
  Includes index.
  ISBN 978-1-4488-7894-9 (library binding) — ISBN 978-1-4488-7982-3 (pbk.) —
ISBN 978-1-4488-7988-5 (6-pack)
  1. Refuse and refuse disposal—Juvenile literature. 2. Recycling (Waste, etc)—Juvenile literature.
I. Title.
  TD792.C56 2013
  628.4'4—dc23
                                   2011050672

Manufactured in the United States of America

CPSIA Compliance Information: Batch #SW12PK: For Further Information contact Rosen Publishing, New York, New York at 1-800-237-9932

THE ENVIRONMENT

WHAT DO WE DO WITH TRASH?

EDWARD CLOSE

PowerKiDS press.

New York

Contents

Talking Trash

When your parents ask you to take out the trash, have you ever wondered where it goes? Trash is anything that people do not want anymore, and they discard it as garbage, which must be disposed of. The United States produces about 250 million tons (227 million t) of trash every day. It is the bigges producer of trash in the world. Trash can affec the environment, so try to be careful about what you do with things you throw away.

Beach pollution
If waste is dumped or washed down drains, it will often end up spilling onto beaches. This can be harmful to marine life and the oceans. Coastal areas around the world that used to be beautiful are now being damaged by beach pollution.

Litter
Throwing a wrapper on the ground may not seem like a big thing. But litter attracts rodents and spoils the look and smell of an area. Animals may get trapped in it or killed by it.

Industrial waste
This is produced by factories, mines, and mills. It includes liquids, sludge, solids, and hazardous waste. If not disposed of properly, it can pollute rivers, lakes, oceans, and forests.

Dangerous waste
Hazardous waste such as chemicals and batteries can harm humans, animals, and the environment.

Types of Trash

All the things we do can produce an enormous amount of different types of trash. Many things can be though of as trash, waste, or garbage. It includes household waste, which comes from people's everyday activities in their homes. It is packaging and old electrical goods, sewage sludge, and building debris. It is garden or plant waste, which is usually called green waste. Waste can be in the form of a liquid, a solid, or a gas. Most of the world's waste comes from households, businesses, industry, construction, and agriculture. Any type of trash can do great harm to the environment if it is not disposed of properly.

Household waste
This includes packaging, food scraps, discarded clothes, an anything else people decide to throw in the trash.

Green waste
This is often made up of garden waste, such as grass clippings, leaves, weeds, and plant cuttin

Industrial waste
This is created by industries. It is more likely to be dangerous waste that must be disposed of properly.

aper
1%

Garden
cuttings
18%

ther
%

Glass and
plastic
15%

etal
%

Food
9%

'hat's in our trash?
st about everything is part of
e garbage: paper, plastics, glass,
od, metals, and garden cuttings.

Paper waste
This is the most common
type of waste. It includes
newspapers, magazines,
and cardboard packaging.

Plastic waste
Many plastic materials, such
as bottles and food packaging,
are thrown away.

rm waste
sticides, fertilizers, and animal
anure are wastes produced
 farming activities.

What Happens to Trash?

There are four main ways that waste is disposed of. It can be buried in a landfill, burned in giant incinerators, recycled into reusable products, or composted at a waste facility. But this depends on what type of waste it is. So it is collected from our homes and transported to a waste disposal site, where it is sorted into different categories of waste.

Dump

Garbage trucks collect trash from curbs all over the city and take it to waste disposal sites, called dumps. Mostly, local or city governments operate the waste disposal site for the community.

RECYCLING CANS

Aluminum cans are 100 percent recyclable. The recycled cans are sorted, crushed, and melted down. The remelted material is used to make new aluminum cans. This produces much less carbon dioxide than if new cans are made with newly smelted aluminum. So, if you recycle a soft drink can, you reduce waste and save energy.

Burning waste

Waste is dumped into furnaces, which are called incinerators or combustors. It is burned at extreme temperatures and produces heat energy, which is sometimes used to generate electricity. The ash that is left is buried in a landfill.

Did You Know?

When trash is burned, it produces gases that pollute Earth's atmosphere. Many incinerators have scrubbers and filters, which clean or reduce the gases that are released into the air.

Landfills

A landfill is a site where waste is buried in a giant hole in the ground. It is the most common method of waste disposal and has been used by many countries around the world for hundreds of years. A landfill buries waste in a way that makes sure it is kept separate from groundwater and does not contaminate the water supply. A landfill also has to make sure that the waste is not in contact with the air and that it is always dry.

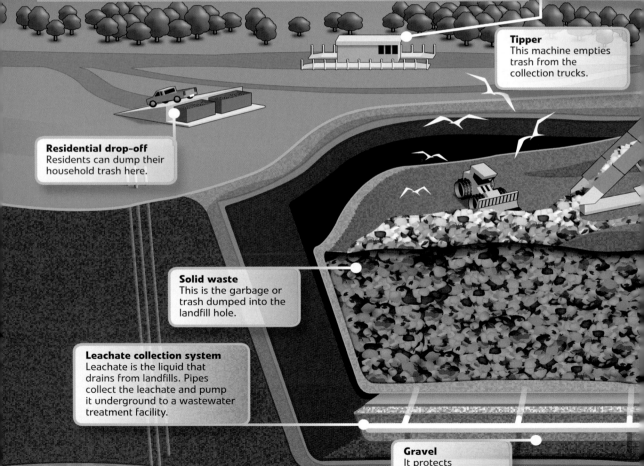

Scale house
Dump trucks are weighed here to find out how much trash they are depositing in the landfill.

Tipper
This machine empties trash from the collection trucks.

Residential drop-off
Residents can dump their household trash here.

Solid waste
This is the garbage or trash dumped into the landfill hole.

Leachate collection system
Leachate is the liquid that drains from landfills. Pipes collect the leachate and pump it underground to a wastewater treatment facility.

Gravel
It protects the leachate collection system.

Anatomy of a landfill

landfill site is not simply about dumping rash in a big hole. Many steps must be aken to ensure that the waste is disposed f safely. This diagram shows the process sed to bury waste in a landfill.

Landfill gas conversion plant
At this facility, gas from the landfill is converted into electricity.

Sediment pond
Surface water runoff flows into ponds, where the sediment settles to the bottom. The clear water is pumped to other water sources.

Dozer
Large machines are needed to spread, crush, and compact the trash.

Sand
This is used as a protective layer for the leachate collection system.

Rear loader
This truck transports trash to the landfill.

Landfill gas extraction system
A vacuum system of wells and pipes extracts gas from the landfill.

What Can We Recycle?

Rubber

Many household items that we throw in the trash can actually be recycled. By sorting the garbage into general trash and recyclable materials, it is possible to cut down the amount of waste as well as save energy and resources. The recyclable materials are taken to a sorting facility, then they are cleaned and made into new products. Many materials are remade into the same products. Materials such as rubber and plastics are made into completely new products.

Plastics

Cardboard

Paper

Glass

Aluminum

RECYCLING PLANT

A recycling plant processes recyclable materials. It uses methods such as melting, shredding, and pulping to break down the materials so they are in a form that can be reused. Once they are broken down, they are shipped to factories that make new products from recycled materials.

Grading glass

Used glass is broken into tiny bits, sorted into different colors, and all paper and metal removed.

Conveyor belt

At a recycling plant, recyclables are sorted on a conveyor belt. Then they are cleaned and made ready for reuse.

Recycling materials

People often separate their recyclable waste from other waste before it is collected. Recycled glass bottles, newspapers, and aluminum cans are remade into the same products.

1

2

Curbside collection
Many cities use large trucks to collect recyclable materials from the curb and transport them to a recycling facility.

Collection containers
You can place paper, bottles, and cans into individual collection containers, which usually have a recycling symbol on them.

Household waste
Recycling is the best way to dispose of newspapers, metal cans, and glass and plastic bottles. It reduces the trash that is dumped in a landfil

How Trash Is Recycled

A complex process is carried out by people and machines to make our used products into materials and products that can be used again. Recycling takes a little extra effort, but it is important to recycle as much as possible. It reduces waste and saves energy. You could have separate containers for recyclable materials in your home. Then, when it is time to put out the trash, the different types of trash will already be sorted and separated.

That's Amazing!
If every American recycled just one tenth of the newspapers that the bought, it would save about 25 millio trees a year. Recycling can conserve natural resources such as forests.

Compacting
The separate piles are compacted into large bundles or put in containers, then taken to a reprocessing plant.

4

orting
the recycling facility, the recyclable aterials are sorted into piles of the me type of material.

Cleaning and remaking
The different bundles of recyclable material are broken down and cleaned, then remade into new products.

5

6

earning
y understanding the benefits and methods of recycling, everyone can educe waste and save energy.

Why Recycle?

As the world's population grows, more and more waste is being produced. Recycling is the best way to reduce the amount of waste that is being dumped in landfills. Reusing products and materials in this way takes less of Earth's natural resources and creates less pollution than making entirely new products does. Making paper from recycled paper can use 50 percent less energy and 90 percent less water than making paper from the pulp of trees. Recycling plastic bottles saves more than 80 percent of the energy needed to make a new plastic bottle. Recycling aluminum cans uses 95 percent less energy than refining and smelting bauxite to make a new can.

Recycling symbol
This symbol is recognized around the world. Any product or packaging that displays it can be recycled.

Landfill gases
As waste breaks down in a landfill, it emits carbon dioxide, methane, and other gases. The gases often have a nasty smell, which spreads to surrounding neighborhoods.

6% Nitrous oxide

9% Chloroflurocarbon

13% Tropospheric ozone

18% Methane

54% Carbon dioxide

Plastic bags

Every year, Americans throw more than 100 billion plastic bags in the trash. Most plastics take hundreds of years to decompose, and bags are a major source of waste pollution. It is estimated they kill more than 100,000 birds, seals, and whales every year.

The Three Rs

Recycling is just one way to cut waste, minimize pollution, conserve resources, and help protect the environment. Other ways to help tackle the problem of waste are to follow the three Rs: reduce, reuse, and rethink. For example, choosing products with less packaging will reduce household waste. Also, many household products and materials can be reused again and again. People are always coming up with new ideas and new ways to minimize waste.

Used book
Take your old books
a secondhand booksto
after you have finishe
reading ther

Did You Know?

When paper is recycled, trees are le
to grow instead of being cut down.
Growing trees absorb carbon dioxid
from the atmosphere, and provide
habitats for plant and animal specie

Disposable containers
Avoid take-out containers by packing your lunch in products that can be used again.

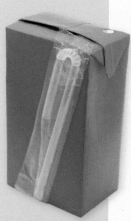

Used clothes
Many resale stores take used clothes. Or you could pass them on to friends or family.

Overpackaging
Use a reusable bottle with a screw-on lid instead of buying disposable drink cartons with straws.

Reduce
Use fewer products. Try to avoid disposable items, and buy only the things that your family really needs.

Small containers
Buy bodycare products in bulk. Some stores let customers bring in empty containers and refill them.

Reuse
Give unused books and clothes t
charity shops. Reuse glass bottle
to store food and other items.

Rethink
Think about how to do things to minimize waste. For example, take your own bags when out shopping.

Compost bin

You can make your own compost bin using old wooden boxes, timber, trash cans, or wire mesh. You can also buy a container specially designed for composting. Then you are ready to start.

1 The container

Decide what type of compost bin you are going to use. Then position it on top of some soil, out of the way in a corner of your yard.

4 Green layer

Add a 2-inch-(5 cm) deep layer of fruit and vegetable scraps, lawn clippings, and green waste material from your garden to the container.

How to make compost

The best way to make compost is to mix layers of vegetable scraps, garden waste, and soil in a container. It takes about three months for this to decompose into a dark, earthy mixture that you put in the garden.

2 The ingredients
You need dead, dried plant material such as fallen leaves. Also use fruit and vegetable skins, lawn clippings, other garden waste, and newspaper.

3 Dry leaf layer
Start by placing a 10-inch-(25 cm) deep layer of dry leaves on the bottom of the container. You can also use sawdust or shredded newspaper in this layer.

5 Soil layer
Cover with a thin layer of soil from the garden. Repeat steps 3 to 5 to use up all the waste material you have and to fill the container if you can.

6 Keep moist
Turn the pile once a week. Check it is moist but not soggy. If it feels dry, add a little water. It should be ready for the garden in three months.

ompost

ood scraps and garden waste make up almost a third of household garbage. Most of it is perfect for making compost, which you use in the garden to make good soil and help plants ow. Organic waste such as old vegetable scraps, lawn clippings, aves, and even weeds are ideal ingredients for compost. So are d newspapers. Adding them to the compost heap instead of the usehold trash cuts the household waste that goes to a landfill.

Helping the Environment

Cleaning products
Many cleaning products contain hazardous chemicals. There are environmentally safer products that use organic materials.

Being part of an environmentally friendly household is th first step you can take in helping to care for the planet. By recycling or reusing as many things as possible and reducing the amount of waste created by your family, you can make a difference. Little things help. Collect rainwater for watering the garden instead of using tap water supplies. Replace old lightbulbs with energy-saving bulbs that use less energy. Another simple way to reduce the amount of energy your home uses is to turn off lights or the television when yo leave the room. Some houses even get their electricity from solar or wind power instead of from burning coal or gas. These are all great ways to help the environment.

Fast-food packaging
Fast-food restaurants in the United States use 1.8 million tons (1.6 million t) of packagir a year. This ends up in a landfill or as litter.

Logging

Forests are logged for the wood to make paper and cardboard. But old newspapers and magazines can be remade into paper products, so fewer trees are cut down. Look out for recycled paper products such as toilet paper at the supermarket.

At school

Schools throughout the world run recycling programs in the school playground. Children sort different types of waste materials in recycling containers, ready to be transported t̲ the recycling depot or drop-off cente̲

ommunity Help

ommunities everywhere are helping to clean up the environment. People join local groups and take part in programs that aim to clean up waste, increase cycling, and reuse household items. Governments run ucation campaigns so people can learn the best ways to cycle and reduce waste at home, school, and work. Many cal areas have recycling depots or drop-off centers, which llect recyclable materials for sorting and making into new oducts. Thrift stores have collection containers on the reet, where used clothes and toys can be taken.

obal cleanup
:h year, about 35 million volunteers m more than 120 countries take rt in Clean Up the World. They work gether to make their neighborhood d our planet a better place to live.

Hazardous waste
Hazardous waste can badly damage the environment. It is important that dangerous chemicals, electrical products, batteries, paints, and oils are disposed of safely.

What You Can Do!

Individuals and families all over the world are taking part in environmentally friendly activities to help reduce waste, and you can, too. It starts in your home and with telling your friends and family about ways to help and contribute. Choose well-made products with little packaging to help reduce waste. Buy products made from recycled materials, because then more products will be remade in the future. Reuse plastic and glass containers so they do not get dumped in a landfill, and avoid using plastic bags if possible.

Recycling
Get involved in a recycling program. Have a container at home for recyclables. Look out for the recycling symbol when shopping.

WORM FARMS

A worm farm is a great way to recycle kitchen vegetable scraps and produce fertilizer for the garden. It does not take up much space and is easy to set up and maintain. Special compost worms break down organic matter. Hardware stores often sell ready-made kits and worms.

Compost worms hard at work

Compost bin
A compost bin recycles kitchen vegetable scraps and garden waste. The compost is good for the garden and it means less waste ends up in a landfill.

Planting
Some countries, such as
Australia, have a national
tree planting day, when
everyone is encouraged to
plant trees in their local area.

Try This For Yourself

Create your own home recycling center. Use this guide to make a recycling center in your house.

1 Find out what can be recycled in your area.

2 Decide how many containers you will need for each kind of recyclable material.

3 Find containers around your house or in your local area.

4 Make designated labels for the containers.

5 Create the space around your house for the containers.

6 Establish a routine you can stick to and keep a checklist.

7 Be mindful when making future purchases and keep an eye out for the recycling symbol.

Glossary

aluminum (uh-LOO-muh-num) A silvery metallic element found n bauxite and often used to make soft drink cans.

bauxite (BOK-syt) A naturally occurring claylike material from which aluminum cans are made.

compost (KOM-pohst) A mixture of decomposed plant and animal material used as garden fertilizer.

contaminate (kun-TA-mih-nayt) To pollute a substance, such as drinking water, or make it impure.

conveyor belt (kun-VAY-er BELT) A belt that transports materials around a factory.

decompose (dee-kum-POHZ) To break down tissues of dead plant or animal matter into simpler forms of material.

fertilizer (FUR-tuh-lyz-er) An agricultural chemical used to improve the soil for growing crops.

groundwater (GROWND-wah-tur) Water that exists beneath Earth's surface in underground streams that can be collected with wells, tunnels, and pipes.

hazardous waste (HA-zer-dus WAYST) Waste that poses a threat to human health or the environment such as toxic, corrosive, or explosive waste. It needs to be disposed of carefully.

household waste (HOWS-hold WAYST) All the trash that is produced in the home, such as food scraps, packaging, and papers.

incinerator (in-SIH-nuh-ray-ter) A furnace used as a waste disposal method by burning waste and reducing it to ashes

industrial waste (in-DUS-tree-ul WAYST) Pollution produced from large industrial plants, including chemical waste and toxic emissions.

landfill (LAND-fil) Also known as a dump; a site for the disposal of waste materials by burial. It is the oldest form of waste treatment.

landfill gases (LAND-fil GAS-ez) Gases created when waste decomposes underground. They are made up primarily of methane and carbon dioxide.

leachate (LEE-chayt) The liquid that drains from landfills.

logging (LOG-ing) The process of cutting down forest trees for timber or land clearing.

manure (muh-NUHR) Organic matter such as plant and animal waste, used as fertilizer on farms.

organic waste (or-GA-nik WAYST) Natural waste that comes from living materials, including vegetable scraps and plant matter.

pesticide (PES-tuh-syd) A chemical sprayed on farm crops to prevent disease or kill pests.

sediment (SEH-deh-ment) The buildup of matter that settles on the bottom of lakes, rivers, and oceans.

solar power (SOH-ler POW-er) Energy from the Sun that is trapped by solar panels and converted into thermal or electrical energy.

wind power (WIND POWER) Electrical energy that is generated by large wind turbines and windmills.

Index

A
aluminum 10, 15, 18
atmosphere 11

B
batteries 8, 27
bauxite 18
burning waste 11

C
carbon dioxide 10, 18, 20
cardboard 14, 25
chemicals 8, 24, 27
compacting 17
compost 22, 23, 28
contaminates 12
conversion plant 12, 13

D
decompose 19, 22

E
extraction system 13

F
farm waste 9
filters 11

G
garden 8, 9, 22–24, 28
glass 9, 15, 16, 20, 28
global cleanup 27
government 10, 27
gravel 12
green waste 8, 22–23
groundwater 12

H
hazardous waste 7, 8, 27
household waste 8, 16, 20, 23

I
incinerator 10, 11
industrial waste 7, 8

L
landfill 10–13, 16, 18, 23, 24, 28
leachate 12, 13
lightbulbs 24
litter 7, 24
logging 25

M
manure 9
methane 18

O
organic waste 23

P
paper 9, 15, 16, 18, 20, 25
pesticide 9
plastic 9, 14, 16, 18, 19, 28

R
rubber 14

S
sand 13
school 26
sediment 13
solar power 24
solid waste 12
supermarket 25

V
vegetable scraps 22, 23, 28

W
wind power 24
World Environment Day 27

Websites

Due to the changing nature of Internet links, PowerKids Press has developed an online list of websites related to the subject of this book. This site is updated regularly. Please use this link to access the list:
www.powerkidslinks.com/disc/trash/